Mother,
I Will Always
Love You

From Bill and Debbie
Mother's Day 1993

Mother, I Will Always Love You

Edited by Susan Polis Schutz

WARNER BOOKS

A Time Warner Company

Warner Books, Inc., 1271 Avenue of the Americas, New York, NY 10020

W A Time Warner Company

Printed in the United States of America

First Printing: May 1990

10 9 8 7 6

Library of Congress Cataloging in Publication Data

Mother, I will always love you / edited by Susan Schutz.
   p. cm.
   ISBN 0-446-39143-3
   1. Mothers—Poetry. 2. American poetry—Women authors.
  3. American poetry—20th century.   I. Schutz, Susan Polis.
  PS595.M64M66 1990
  811'.540803520431—dc20

CONTENTS

Every Day of My Life...
I Love You, Mother

When I was little,
you were always there
when I needed you.
If I was wrong, you told me,
but you also stood beside me.
Your love and support
were steady and strong.

There were times
when we did not agree,
but I always knew your love for me
guided you in your decisions.
Now that I am older,
your love and support
are just as important to me.
I need you as much as I ever have,
and knowing you are there is
a constant source of comfort to me.

You are more than my mother;
you are my very dearest friend.

— Linda Denninger

Mother, I Thank You Forever for Our Relationship

*F*or as long as I can remember
you were always by my side
to give me support
to give me confidence
to give me help

For as long as I can remember
you were always the person
    I looked up to
so strong
so sensitive
so pretty

For as long as I can remember
and still today
you are everything
a mother should be

For as long as I can remember
you always provided stability
within our family
full of laughter
full of tears
full of love

So much of what I have become
is because of you
and I thank you
forever
for our
relationship

— Susan Polis Schutz

You Are the
Best Mother of All

If I had to pick one thing
   about you, Mother,
that makes you so special,
I don't think it would be possible.
I couldn't begin to count
the number of times
you tolerated my moods,
consoled my heartbreaks
   and disappointments,
endured my ups and downs,
listened to words confused by tears,
and just simply understood
for no other reason
than because you love me.
The years hold precious memories,
but most of all, they hold growth.
In a way, we grew up together.
There's still some growing left to do,
but one thing becomes more clear to me
with each passing day,
and I hope you know:
there's no other mother like you,
and I love you very much.

— Susan M. Pavlis

Mother, I Will Always Love You
Much More than You Will Ever Know

*In my solitary moments, Mother,
I often take the time to reflect on you,
and I realize that being a mother
is a lifelong commitment to selflessness.
I think that motherhood must be
the most difficult commitment to pursue,
as more often than not, it requires
much more giving than receiving.
The rewards of this commitment
seem to be so very few,
and the demands so very great.
Few children, and I am one of them,
ever take the opportunity to view
the realities of motherhood.
Oftentimes, I am so caught up
in my own life that I fail to realize
that I am never alone in any emotion.
For each moment of joy I experience,
there is a silent joy shared by you,
my mother, along with a silent prayer
of thanks to God for the blessing
He has given me, your child.*

Behind each tear shed and each hurt felt,
there is a silent tear and a silent hurt
felt deep inside your heart.
It's strange that these silent emotions
are never readily apparent,
but they are always behind your words
of encouragement, wisdom, understanding,
and faith that there will be
a better tomorrow awaiting me.
I also have silent emotions;
mine are the prayers of thanks to God
that I hold deep within my heart
whenever I reflect upon you, my mother.
I will always love you much more
than you will ever know.

— Catherine I. DiGiorgio

I Love You Forever, Mother

You have shown me how to give of myself
You have shown me leadership
You have taught me to be strong
You have taught me
  the importance of the family
You have demonstrated unconditional love
You have demonstrated a sensitivity
  to people's needs
You have handed down to me the important
  values in life
You have handed down to me the idea of
  achieving one's goals
You have set an example, throughout your life
of what a mother and woman should be like
I am so proud of you
and I love you
forever

— Susan Polis Schutz

You Will Always Be
the Person I Turn To

*M*other, there are times
when I need a friend to talk to,
but every friend I can think of
just isn't the right person
for the mood I am in.
My usual friends
who understand and care about me
just aren't the ones I want
to listen to my problems;
I need you.
You are the one
who can really understand me
and who can make me feel better
just by hearing your voice.
I remember so many times
when I came to you in tears
about life's unfair situations
and disappointments;
you always listened.

I remember telling you
how lonely and unhappy I felt,
and you always told me
how much you loved me
and how special I was.
You always knew I was strong enough
to get through my troubles.
And though my friends
have helped me at times
to get through the changes,
you are the only one in my life
who I know will be there for me
any time of the day or night,
and understand exactly how I feel.
You are not only my loving mother;
you truly are my very best friend.

— Laura Medley

I Wish There Weren't
So Many Miles Between Us

I wish there weren't
so many miles between us,
because I would love to spend
    more time with you.
Even though we're apart,
I send my love
and share my thoughts with you.
I am so proud to have you
    as my mother,
and as I remember your guidance
    from my childhood days
until adulthood,
I not only recall the warm memories
    we have shared,
but the love we have always had
    for one another
and the need I have for you
    in my life.
Thank you for always being there
    when I need you,
and for being the wonderful
    mother you are.

— Susan J. Sater

No Words Could Ever Express
My Love for You

*Looking back,
I can see so many sacrifices
you made along the way.
Some were small, and some
    were too great to repay,
but they were all made
without hesitation —
    because you loved me.*

*As I think of all my yesterdays,
I recall so many times when you
turned my tears into laughter,
so many problems
you helped me to face.*

*You were a shoulder to lean on
when I needed you;
you were always there —
    because you loved me.*

As I grew older,
you couldn't always be with me,
but you always were there in spirit,
giving guidance when I needed it,
helping me make each decision.
You taught me to be strong
and to believe in myself.
You taught me right from wrong —
    because you loved me.

Now, I look back on the years
and realize how lucky I have been.
You were and are a very special
part of my life.
I want to thank you for helping me
become the person I am now,
for giving me the courage
to reach for my dreams.
My life is rich and my heart is full
because of you.
I love you, too.

— Deanne Laura Gilbert

To My Mother

When you have a mother
who cares so much for you
that anything you want
comes before her desires
When you have a mother
who is so understanding that
no matter what is bothering you
she can make you smile
When you have a mother
who is so strong that
no matter what obstacles she faces
she is always confident in front of you
When you have a mother
who actively pursues her goals in life
but includes you in all her goals
you are very lucky indeed
Having a mother like this
makes it easy to grow up
into a loving, strong adult
Thank you for
being this kind
of wonderful
mother

— Susan Polis Schutz

Mother, I'll Always Need You in My Life

When I was born, I was glad
you were there to hold me
and comfort me,
to feed me and rock me to sleep.
As I grew, I was glad
you were there to make our house
feel like a home.
When I was a teenager, I was glad
you were there to talk to me
when things weren't going quite right;
you would tell me it would be okay.
I am glad you've always been there
to encourage me to do my best
in whatever I do.
You've been there to reassure me
at times in my life when
it was so hard to find the answers.
And I'm glad you always forgave me
for the arguments that it seems
most children have with their mother.

*Now that I'm grown, I've realized
that all the wise decisions you made
over the years have helped me
become the person I am.
The love you gave me, the trust,
discipline, and understanding
were exactly what I needed to grow.
I find that I appreciate you
even more than I did when I was little,
because I know now what
a difficult job it is to be
the kind of mother you are.
And even though I'm not little anymore,
I still need you, Mother.
I still come to you to talk, laugh,
and even cry about this world and life.
At every time in my life,
I need you and love you more than ever.*

— Sharon Johnson O'Donnell

Mother, You Mean
So Much to Me

There are so many words
I could try to say to you
to let you know
how much you mean to me,
but really
the two most important feelings
I want you to know are . . .

"Thank you"
for all your love,
and
"I love you"
with all my heart.

— Deanna Beisser

Thank You
for Everything
You've Taught Me

Mother, you have sacrificed
a lot for me,
and I want to say thank you
for teaching and guiding me
through all my years
    of childhood.
Your guidance has helped me
choose right from wrong.
By your discipline
    and praise,
you made me a more confident
and secure person.
Whenever things got tough,
you were always there for me
    when I needed you,
and I thank you.

By all the nights
you stayed up with me
   when I was sick,
or waited for me
   to come home,
you helped me learn compassion.
By being there for me,
you have not only been
   my mother;
you have become my friend.
I love you,
   and I want you to know
that I couldn't have
   a better mother.
Thank you, Mother.
I love you.

— *Sharon McCorkle*

I Love You, My Ideal Mother

Every day
I think about you with such pride
You seem to be getting younger
and more energetic
You seem to have accomplished
  more than ever

Every day
I think about you with such respect
You do everything so gracefully
You are always more than ready to help
  anyone in our family
You seem to have given
  more of yourself than ever

Every day
I want you to know that
I love you so much
as a great person
and as an ideal mother

— Susan Polis Schutz

Everyone Needs Someone
like You, Mother

*E*veryone needs someone to think
that they are special.
For me, that someone is you, Mother.

Everyone needs someone who is
always there and always caring.
Everyone needs someone who is just a
touch or a card or a phone call away.
Someone with whom you can share
everything that's in your heart
or simply talk about the day
in the way that only the two of you can.

Everyone needs someone to encourage them;
to believe in them; to give a pat on
the back when things have gone right,
and a shoulder to cry on when they haven't.
Everyone needs someone to remind them
to keep trying and that it will all work out.

Everyone needs someone like you; I know that
so well. Because I know how very much I've
needed you and cherished you all these years.
And I know that I could never love anyone
in the same sweet, precious way
   that I will always love you, Mother.

I hope everyone has someone
   who's as wonderful as you.

— Laurel Atherton

Mother, Your Love Is a Special Part of My Life

Mother, so many times you set aside
your own worries and problems
to listen and care about mine.
More times than I could ever count,
you have given me hope
and revived my goals and dreams.
Every moment, I am aware
   of your value to me,
and I appreciate those times
when I have the chance
   to let you know
how much I love you.

— Ann Rudacille

Thank You, Mother

I want to apologize
for any problems
that I may have caused you
in the past
I am not
the easiest person
to live with
since I am so
independent and strong
but you can be sure
that though it possibly
didn't seem like it
your values and ideals
did pass on to me
and I carry them forward
in all that I do

You always were someone
stable, strong, giving and warm
an ideal person to look up to
This has given me the
strength to lead
my own life
according to my own standards
Your leadership and love
have enabled me to grow
into a very
happy person
and I think that is
what every mother wishes
for her child
Thank you

— Susan Polis Schutz

I'm Grateful to Have
a Mother like You

A mother like you must be
the dearest of all God's creations.

*I can't think of anything
that is as sweet
    as a mother's love,
that is as precious
    as you are to me,
or that is as appreciated
    as you are by every single smile
        within me.*

*I love you so much, Mother.
And I thank God that you're mine.*

— Carey Martin

Mother, I Love You
More than Words Can Say

You have always been the
light of my life.
It seems like I've been telling
people about you ever since
I began to talk.
But I'm not sure I ever
really found the right words
to say to you.

Mother, you are what love is
and what beauty can be.
You are what kindness and goodness
should always be like.

You're an image of open arms
*   and a gentle smile that I can't think of*
*   without tears coming to my eyes.*
In so many ways, I am closer to you
*   than to anyone else, and it makes me*
*   so glad to know that's how it will*
*   always be.*

I can't imagine that anyone could have
a more wonderful mother than the one
*   you have always been to me.*

— Laurel Atherton

You Always Were
Someone to Look Up To

Since I had a mother
whose many interests
kept her excited and occupied

Since I had a mother
who interacted with so many people
that she had a real feeling for the world

Since I had a mother
who always was strong
through any period of suffering

Since I had a mother
who was a complete person
I always had a model
to look up to
and that made it easier
for me to develop into
an independent woman

— Susan Polis Schutz

I'm the Person I Am Today
Because of Your Love

*I*t is because of your love
that I am the person I am today.
When I was growing up,
you were always there for me.
You gave up so much to be a mother.
My needs were anticipated
    and met.
Nothing ever came before me.
And no matter how silly
some of my problems were,
you listened to me
and taught me to make
    intelligent choices.

Between your love and patience,
I've grown to become
a confident, responsible person.
By your example, I have learned
to respect every person's right
to live their own life,
by your giving me respect for mine.

In my eyes, Mother, you are the best.
I love you.

— Kathryn Ardanowski

My Ideal Mother

An ideal mother should be
strong and guiding
understanding and giving
An ideal mother should be
honest and forthright
confident and able
An ideal mother should be
relaxed and soft
flexible and tolerant
But most of all
an ideal mother should be a
loving woman
who is always there when needed
and who
by being happy and satisfied
with herself
is able to be happy and loving
with her children
Mother, you are a rare woman—
you are everything an
ideal mother should be

— Susan Polis Schutz

Dear Mother . . . I Love You

No matter how much I do
that disappoints you,
no matter how often I forget
all you do for me,
your heart is always open.

You have given me more than life;
you have taught me how
to believe in myself
and strive for my dreams.

You have supported
my decisions,
although in your heart you knew
they were not always the best.

And if I failed, you awaited me
  with open arms,
as if I could do no wrong,
helping me to grow and learn,
to find the strength to go on
and become a better person.

You have taught me
  to never give up hope
and always to remember those
  who may not be as fortunate
  as me.
Dear Mother, I love you.

— Helena Bewley

Mother, This Thank-You Is for All the Ones I Never Said

Mother, I didn't always realize
that you had dreams of your own.
Like many children,
there was a time when I thought
your whole purpose in life
was just to be my mother.
During my childhood
   and teenage years,
I didn't always consider
your feelings or needs.
I never wondered if you ever
felt lonely when I was engrossed
with my own interests and friends,
or if you felt unappreciated
when my thanks were too
   infrequently expressed.
I never considered that
worries, disappointments,
   or sadnesses
could touch your life;
I was too involved
   with my own problems
to be sensitive to yours,
or to take the time
   to say what I want to today —
   that I couldn't love you more.

— Ann Rudacille

Thank You for Teaching Me About Life

Mother, whenever I set aside
some time to consider
all that I am thankful for,
you're always the first one
   who comes to mind.
You were the first one
to welcome me into this world;
the first one I came to for
every hurt or broken heart;
the first to smile when I did well,
and the first to gently comfort me
when I didn't.
You were the first person
to teach me about love, kindness,
and believing in dreams,
and those lessons have stayed
with me all my life.

— Edmund O'Neill

Mother, I Have a Wish Especially for You

Mother,
may you be blessed
with an abundance
of happiness;
may you find peace
in all that you do;
may love
be with you always,
and may the joys
you cherish
be a part
of each day of your life.

— *Deanne Laura Gilbert*

There's a Part of You
in Everything I Do

I have grown
to understand you
as my mother
and as my friend.

A part of you
comes through in me
with every relationship I have,
every problem I come across,
and every decision I make.
I have tried to put in myself
all that I admire in you.

I have watched you
at all times,
so that I may one day handle
happiness and crises
the way you do.

No one could be
a better mother
*   than you are,*
and no one could
ever love their mother
more than I love you.

— Marcelle Soviero

Mother, No Words or Gifts
Can Express All My Love for You

Within my life, Mother,
you have given me so much.
There are no words or gifts
that could ever express all my love.
I wish I could give you all the things
you have given me.
You helped me when I thought
    there was no hope.
I admire you and the confidence you show;
no matter how bad things get,
you always manage to pull through.
You've been a good teacher
    for me to learn from and follow.
You stand back and let me make
    the mistakes I need to
in order to grow.

You show me different sides
to every situation,
letting me come to my own conclusions.
I'm able to talk to you about anything,
without fear of being misunderstood.
You're always willing to give me
another chance,
and encourage me even when I fail.
Nothing can ever take the place
you hold in my heart;
I love you as my mother,
but most of all, as my friend.

— Cheryl Gray

Mother, I Love and Appreciate You Forever

I have gone through
so many different stages
changing ideas and goals
while searching for the
right kind of life for me
You were always
ready to help me
at all times
It must have seemed like
I would never
follow one straight path
Now that I know
what I am doing and
where I am going
I can only show you
my extreme appreciation
for your support
by being true
to the ideals and values
that you tried to teach me
Thank you forever
for standing by me
I love and appreciate
you forever

— Susan Polis Schutz

My Dearest Mother

I love you, Mother.
You have always been to me
a blessing and an inspiration,
giving me security within your love.
I know that
I do not always follow the path
that you might choose.
I realize how much you wish to save me
from the hurt of life,
wishing for me to make only wise choices.
Your pride in me is one of my
most valued treasures,
and when you are disappointed in me,
I hurt, too.
You have taught me through love and
experience
those things that make me who I am
and give me the strength to believe
in myself.
You have shown me my ability to fulfill
that potential we all have.

I may not always choose the easy path,
    and I may sometimes be wrong,
but I have learned to make my own
    decisions, based on what I believe
        is right at the time —
realizing that time may change my
    decision.
Though you may not always understand
    my actions or my deeds,
please know in your heart and soul
that you, dearest Mother,
are important to me.
Regardless of the path I walk,
I will always respect your judgment,
though I may not always accept it as
    my own.
I love you, Mother,
and I only hope that I can give to
    others as much of myself
        as you have given of yourself to me.

— *Teresa L. Cornett*

ACKNOWLEDGMENTS

We gratefully acknowledge the permission granted by the following authors to reprint their works.

Laura Medley for "You Will Always Be the Person I Turn To."

Susan J. Sater for "I Wish There Weren't So Many Miles Between Us."

Deanne Laura Gilbert for "No Words Could Ever Express My Love for You."

Sharon Johnson O'Donnell for "Mother, I'll Always Need You in My Life."

Ann Rudacille for "Mother, Your Love Is a Special Part of My Life" and "Mother, This Thank-You Is for All the Ones I Never Said."

Kathryn Ardanowski for "I'm the Person I Am Today Because of Your Love."

Helena Bewley for "Dear Mother. . .I Love You."

Marcelle Soviero for "There's a Part of You in Everything I Do."